THE POWER OF A

WHISPER

PARTICIPANT'S GUIDE

D1114577

Books by Bill Hybels

Axiom
Holy Discontent
Just Walk Across the Room
The Volunteer Revolution
Courageous Leadership
Rediscovering Church (with Lynne Hybels)
Honest to God?
Fit to be Tied (with Lynne Hybels)
Descending into Greatness (with Rob Wilkins)
Becoming a Contagious Christian (with Mark Mittelberg and Lee Strobel)

The New Community Series
(with Kevin and Sherry Harney)

Colossians
James
1 Peter
Philippians
Romans
The Sermon on the Mount 1
The Sermon on the Mount 2

The InterActions Small Group Series
(with Kevin and Sherry Harney)

Authenticity
Character
Commitment
Community
Essential Christianity
Fruit of the Spirit
Getting a Grip
Jesus
Lessons on Love
Living in God's Power

Love in Action
Marriage
Meeting God
New Identity
Parenting
Prayer
Reaching Out
The Real Deal
Significance
Transformation

THE POWER OF A
WHISPER

HEARING GOD. HAVING THE GUTS TO RESPOND.

PARTICIPANT'S GUIDE
Four Sessions

BILL HYBELS

with Ashley Wiersma

ZONDERVAN®

ZONDERVAN.com/
AUTHORTRACKER
follow your favorite authors

ZONDERVAN

The Power of a Whisper Participant's Guide
Copyright © 2010 by Bill Hybels

Requests for information should be addressed to:

Zondervan, Grand Rapids, Michigan 49530

ISBN 978-0-310-32948-0

Cover photography: Getty Images / Guy Edwardes
Interior design: Beth Shagene

Printed in the United States of America

10 11 12 13 14 15 /DCI/ 23 22 21 20 19 18 17 16 15 14 13 12 11 10 9 8 7 6 5 4 3 2 1

CONTENTS

READ THIS FIRST

If you are looking for something super-personal,
then it is not a question of choosing between
the Christian idea and the other ideas.
The Christian idea is the only one on the market.

C. S. Lewis

WELCOME TO *THE POWER OF A WHISPER* FOUR-SESSION journey toward getting better at hearing from God and getting bolder about obeying what he asks us to do. You're in for quite a ride as you explore what it means to let input from heaven navigate your life here on earth! Before you dive in, skim the following notes, which will set you up for success in your small-group setting.

Group Preparation

Whether your small group has been meeting together for years or is convening for the first time to engage with this curriculum, be sure to designate a consistent time and place to work through the four sessions that follow. For example, consider meeting for an hour on four consecutive Tuesday mornings or Wednesday evenings or Sunday afternoons at a local coffee shop, in a group member's living room, at a nearby park or in a common gathering area at your church.

Once you establish the when and where of your times together, select a facilitator who will keep discussions on track and an eye on the clock. If you choose to rotate this responsibility, assign the four sessions to their respective facilitators upfront, so that group members can prepare their thoughts and questions prior to the session they are responsible for leading.

A Note to Facilitators

As facilitator, you are responsible for honoring the sixty-minute timeframe of each meeting, for catalyzing helpful discussion among your group, and for keeping the dialogue equitable by drawing out quieter members and helping more talkative members to remember that others' insights are valued in your group.

You might find it helpful to preview each session's video teaching segment and then scan the "Group Discussion" questions that pertain to it, highlighting various questions that you want to be sure to cover during your group's meeting. Ask God in advance of your time together to guide your group's discussion, and then be sensitive to the direction he wishes to lead.

Session Format

Each session includes five parts that are intended for the small-group experience:

- **Opening prayer** [allow 3 minutes] — words to help you devote your group time to God

- **"Getting Going" question** [allow 5 minutes] — a simple icebreaker that relates to the session topic and invites input from every group member as the meeting begins

- **Video-based teaching** [allow 20–25 minutes] — practical help from pastor and author Bill Hybels regarding how to hear from God and how to meticulously obey the instruction you receive

- **Group discussion** [allow 25–30 minutes] — questions and exercises that reinforce the session content and elicit personal input from every group member

- **"Giving the Whisper-Led Life a Try" challenge** [allow 2 minutes] — an easy-to-implement opportunity to practice the ideas introduced during each session before your group convenes again

Additionally, you will find an "Individual Reflection" segment at the end of each session that includes a recap of the content covered, as well as questions and exercises for group members to explore on their own between group meetings.

Prior to each session, group members will be encouraged to read two to three chapters from Bill Hybels's hardcover book, *The Power of a Whisper: Hearing God, Having the Guts to Respond* (Zondervan, 2010). While these readings certainly help flesh out participants' understanding of the concepts covered in each session's video segment, they shouldn't be considered prerequisites to engaging in group discussions.

Hopefully, you and your group will discover inspiring stories, practical teaching points and helpful discussion starters throughout each of the four sessions. Enjoy the glimpse into what a whisper-led life can look like when God's people prioritize hearing from heaven and following the direction they receive!

Personal Preparation

Referring to the relationship between devoted followers of Christ and their Good Shepherd, Jesus said, "My sheep listen to my voice" (John 10:27).[1] If there is one goal for this four-session experience, it is precisely that — that you would learn to pick out the voice of God from the cacophony of other voices vying for your attention each day. And then, that you would choose to obey.

If you share this goal, then commit now that for all four sessions, you will be still, you will push aside other priorities, you will seek to engage this content with your full attention and you will focus on hearing from God — frequently, consistently and intimately.

Practically, you'll want to bring the following items to each group meeting:

• Your Bible

• Your copy of the book, *The Power of a Whisper: Hearing God, Having the Guts to Respond*

• This participant's guide and a pen

Rest assured that your earnest preparation for and serious devotion to this experience will yield great things in your life. "Trust in the LORD with all your heart and lean not on your own understanding; in all your ways acknowledge him," Proverbs 3:5–6 promises, "and he will make your paths straight." What a thrill it is to know that when you allow God to guide your steps, those steps will fall on a perfectly straight path.

Let the whisper-led journey begin!

SEIZING YOUR
"MISS VAN SOELEN" MOMENT

BY BILL HYBELS

THE FIRST ACKNOWLEDGMENT IN MY BOOK, *THE POWER OF A WHISPER*, went to my second-grade teacher, Miss Van Soelen. Decades ago, she was the one who taught a Bible story to my class of seven-year-olds about Samuel, a young boy who heard voices in the middle of the night. As the story went, Samuel would get out of bed, go find his mentor, Eli, and say, "You called me?" To which Eli would say, "I didn't call you. Go back to bed."[2]

This happened three times, and finally Eli said to Samuel, "Next time you hear a voice, say, 'Speak, Lord, your servant is listening.'"

So, obedient child that he was, Samuel went back to bed; he heard the voice again and dutifully said, "Speak, Lord, your servant is listening."

Amazingly, God actually spoke. He spoke a very important message to young Samuel that he was to convey to Eli the following day.

Miss Van Soelen finished telling that story one afternoon just as the recess bell rang. The sound of that bell usually launched me from my seat and out the door in a matter of seconds, but that day, as all of my classmates rushed out, I sat transfixed at my small wooden desk.

I was glued to my chair because of the nature of that story, a story of the King of the entire universe actually *speaking* to someone on earth.

Very timidly, after all of the other kids had made their way outside, I walked to the front of the classroom and said, "Miss Van Soelen, does God still speak to little boys today?"

She looked me right in the eye and said, *"Absolutely*, God still speaks."

Just then, she reached into the top drawer of her desk, pulled out a slip of paper, and handed it to me. She said, "I've been keeping this here, but maybe you'd like to have it now, based on what we just talked about ..."

I said thanks, jabbed the folded-up piece of paper into my pants pocket and headed outside to play.

Later that night, just before I climbed into bed, I reached for those pants and pulled out the crumpled piece of paper. On it was written a poem — a poem I liked so much that I decided to memorize it.

The next day, I went to school. Once that afternoon's Bible story had come and gone and the recess bell had rung, Miss Van Soelen caught me midstride as I rushed to the baseball field. "Did you read that poem I gave you?" she asked.

I told my teacher that not only had I read it, but that I had committed it to memory, a fact I thought might cause her to faint then and there. "You *did?*" she asked, shock written all over her face.

She challenged me to recite the poem, and I did:

Oh! give me Samuel's ear,
An open ear, O Lord,
Alive and quick to hear
Each whisper of Thy Word;
Like him to answer to Thy call
And to obey Thee first of all.[3]

The look on Miss Van Soelen's face when I finished my recitation was priceless. With a pride-filled grin on her face, she placed her heavy hands on my small shoulders and said, "Billy Hybels, if you listen for the voice of God and obey it, I think he will not only speak to you throughout your days, but he will also infuse your life with *great* power."

Since those boyhood days, I have repeated that little poem perhaps tens of thousands of times. And it has called me to new levels of obedience every time.

Several weeks ago, I received an advance copy of the book, *The Power of a Whisper*, from my publisher. As I held that book in my hand and saw the near-final version for the first time, I thought, "This entire thing traces all the way back to an ordinary afternoon in the second grade, when Miss Van Soelen introduced me to the idea that God really does speak to his children ... and that if I'm careful to learn to hear his voice, he might even speak to me."

Right then, as the thought was still spinning through my mind, my assistant stepped into my office holding a printed copy of an email she had just received and said, "Bill, you'd better sit down. I have some bad news."

I sat down as the words formed on her lips: "Your second-grade teacher has died ..."

She handed me the piece of paper, and as I held my new book

in one hand and that disheartening news in the other, I marveled at the timing of life.

My schedule was filled to the brim with appointments, both that day and the next, but a whisper from God came through, loud and clear. "Attend her funeral," he seemed to say. "Cancel what you need to cancel, and get to her hometown today."

I thought about it, I prayed about it and I decided that's exactly what I would do.

As I stood by Miss Van Soelen's casket the following morning, I considered how one five-minute conversation with one caring woman changed the course of my entire life. Silently and reverently, I thanked her for the immeasurable impact she'd had on me, and as I drove away from that funeral, I rededicated myself to the idea of living with one ear open to heaven each and every day.

Part of the reason I am so passionate about the curriculum you are about to explore is that I believe a "Miss Van Soelen" moment is awaiting you, an occasion when you come face to face with the undeniable truth that God still speaks to his children, and that, most likely, he is wanting to speak to you. Ready to find out if I'm right?

South Haven, Michigan
April 2010

THE WHISPER-LED LIFE

The knowledge that we are never alone
calms the troubled sea of our lives
and speaks peace to our souls.
A. W. Tozer

What to Expect, Session 1

In this session, you'll be introduced to Gerry Couchman, a man who is living a whisper-led life, and invited to join him in the greatest adventure Christ-followers can know: allowing input from heaven to direct their journey here on earth. To prepare for session 1, skim the following three chapters from Bill Hybels's *The Power of a Whisper: Hearing God, Having the Guts to Respond*:

- 📖 Ch. 1, "Samuel's Ear"
- 📖 Ch. 4, "How to Know When You're Hearing from God"
- 📖 Ch. 10, "Just Say the Word"

Opening Prayer

Focus your group on devoting this hour to God by praying the prayer below.

"God, thank you for your willingness to speak into our hearts, our days and our lives. As we focus on what a whisper-led life might look like over the course of this next hour, we give you full permission to challenge and convict us, as well as to comfort us with your unparalleled care. Thanks for being here with us today. Amen."

Getting Going

As your group prepares to view this session's video content, briefly share your response to the following question:

What is one of the most memorable things God has ever prompted you to do?

Video Notes

In the space below, record your observations regarding this session's video, as well as any personal promptings God lays on your mind and heart.

"The awareness of God's presence in your life is the most transformative knowledge there is."
Bill Hybels

Group Discussion

After viewing the session 1 video, answer the questions that follow in full group.

1. First things first: What stood out to you regarding Gerry Couchman's kidney-donation story?

2. Gerry described two specific whispers that he has received along the way — one to donate his kidney and one to persevere in his work serving local-church pastors. Can you relate? How frequently is your life guided by "divine input from above"?

3. How do you determine when a whisper you receive is really from God? What does your "whisper test" typically include?

4. Following Gerry's story, Bill Hybels mentioned five "filters" he uses to discern whether the voice he is sensing is God's. If you were to receive a divine nudge or prompting today regarding a pressing situation you face, which of these test-questions would you be most likely to ask, and which might you neglect to explore? Explain why to your group.

- ☐ "God, is this prompting truly from you?"
- ☐ "Is the whisper scriptural?"
- ☐ "Is it wise?"
- ☐ "Is it in tune with my own character or wiring?"
- ☐ "What do the people I most trust think about it?"

"There is an intimate relationship between the Shepherd and the sheep which is always initiated by the Shepherd himself. But there is something for the sheep to do when he enters the fold. He has to be willing to hear and respond to the Shepherd's voice."

Rosalind Rinker

5. What does a person stand to gain by learning to slow down and *thoroughly* test every whisper he or she receives?

6. Tucked in the middle of Isaiah 30, a chapter that lays out a litany of tough condemnations against a people group that refused to listen to God, is this inspiring verse: "Whether you turn to the right or to the left, your ears will hear a voice behind you, saying, 'This is the way; walk in it'" (Isaiah 30:21).

   As you consider improving your "spiritual hearing" during these next few sessions, what does a promise like that from God mean to you?

7. For Gerry Couchman, the "way" in which he was asked to walk involved great personal and physical sacrifice. How willing would you be to walk in the way God leads you, even if physical, financial, emotional, vocational or some other form of sacrifice on your part was required?

8. Toward the end of this session's video, Bill Hybels said, "God is looking for 'just say the word' Christ-followers, women and men who will do *whatever* it takes to follow the promptings they receive." The idea is based on the story from Matthew 8:5–13 of the centurion who asked Jesus to heal the soldier's servant (see chapter 10 of *The Power of a Whisper*, which you read in preparation for this week's session).

   Based on your life experience thus far, how open have you been to following divine input from above? Place an "X" on the continuum at the top of the next page, and then explain your rationale for that placement to the group.

Before now, I'd never really considered that God was speaking to me.

I listen for God's whispers every day and try to do exactly what he asks.

9. Regardless of where you may find yourself on the "just say the word" spectrum above, what words of reassurance does Isaiah 58:11 offer you today? (See shaded box for text.)

"I will always show you where to go. I'll give you a full life in the emptiest of places — firm muscles, strong bones. You'll be like a well-watered garden, a gurgling spring that never runs dry."

Isaiah 58:11 (MSG)

Giving the Whisper-Led Life a Try

Agree to engage in the following activity before your group meets for session 2 and to come to that meeting prepared to discuss your experience.

Bill Hybels closed this week's video with an invitation to live with a "higher goal," the goal of never wanting to miss another whisper from God for the rest of our lives.

Between now and when your group meets again, get alone before your heavenly Father and ask him to help you prioritize the "higher" goal of hearing from him. On the grid that follows, note the three or four aspirations that are top-of-mind for you these days. Then, beside each, jot down a few questions that invite God to speak into that goal (an example has been provided). Also, as you interact with your heavenly Father, pay attention to goals that he may be asking you to set aside for now, as well as new ones he prompts you to add to your list.

My Current Goals	Questions I Have of God
[example] Get out of debt.	• How am I supposed to tithe, when money is this tight? • What needs should go unmet while I work to get out of debt? • What do you want me to learn through this process? • In what ways should my lifestyle shift, once I'm finally out of debt?

My Current Goals	Questions I Have of God

Take time before your next small-group meeting to pose your questions before God. Ask him for timely, divine input, and in the space below, note the input that you receive in reply.

INDIVIDUAL REFLECTION
SESSION 1

Before you meet with your group for session 2, take some time on your own to review and pray through the big ideas from this session's content as well as the Sitting with the Subject Matter section that follows.

The Big Ideas

- God promises in Isaiah 30 that even today his followers can and will hear his voice saying, "This is the way; walk in it."

- As you learn to hear from God, these five questions will help you discern whether a whisper truly was heaven-sent:

  1. "God, is this prompting truly from you?"

  2. "Is the whisper scriptural?"

  3. "Is it wise?"

  4. "Is it in tune with my own character or wiring patterns?"

  5. "What do the people I most trust think about it?"

- Like the centurion whose story is told in Matthew 8, God is looking for women and men who have a "just say the word" posture toward obeying the whispers they receive, even when those promptings require personal sacrifice.

Sitting with the Subject Matter

READ: *1 Kings 19:1–13*

First Kings 19:1–13 (see shaded box) details the story of the prophet Elijah hearing God's voice not in a mighty wind, an earthquake or a raging fire, but in what the text calls a "gentle whisper."

"Now Ahab told Jezebel everything Elijah had done and how he had killed all the prophets with the sword. So Jezebel sent a messenger to Elijah to say, 'May the gods deal with me, be it ever so severely, if by this time tomorrow I do not make your life like that of one of them.'

"Elijah was afraid and ran for his life. When he came to Beersheba in Judah, he left his servant there, while he himself went a day's journey into the desert. He came to a broom tree, sat down under it and prayed that he might die. 'I have had enough, LORD,' he said. 'Take my life; I am no better than my ancestors.' Then he lay down under the tree and fell asleep.

"All at once an angel touched him and said, 'Get up and eat.' He looked around, and there by his head was a cake of bread baked over hot coals, and a jar of water. He ate and drank and then lay down again.

"The angel of the LORD came back a second time and touched him and said, 'Get up and eat, for the journey is too much for you.' So he got up and ate and drank. Strengthened by that food, he traveled forty days and forty nights until he reached Horeb, the mountain of God. There he went into a cave and spent the night. And the word of the LORD came to him: 'What are you doing here, Elijah?'

"He replied, 'I have been very zealous for the LORD God

Almighty. The Israelites have rejected your covenant, broken down your altars, and put your prophets to death with the sword. I am the only one left, and now they are trying to kill me too.'

"The LORD said, 'Go out and stand on the mountain in the presence of the LORD, for the LORD is about to pass by.'

"Then a great and powerful wind tore the mountains apart and shattered the rocks before the LORD, but the LORD was not in the wind. After the wind there was an earthquake, but the LORD was not in the earthquake. After the earthquake came a fire, but the LORD was not in the fire. And after the fire came a gentle whisper. When Elijah heard it, he pulled his cloak over his face and went out and stood at the mouth of the cave."

1 Kings 19:1–13

REFLECT: *When have you heard the "gentle whisper" of God in your own life?*

In *The Power of a Whisper: Hearing God, Having the Guts to Respond*, Bill Hybels says, "We serve a communicating God — a God of words. [Throughout Scripture, he] created with a word, he healed with a word, he encouraged with a word, he rebuked with a word, he guided with a word, he prophesied with a word, he assured with a word, he loved with a word, he served with a word and he comforted with a word. Throughout all of history, God has communicated, and he still is at it today. The issue isn't whether or not God is speaking; it's whether we will have ears to hear what he says."[4]

In Bill's own life, as he mentioned in this session's video segment, God's "low-volume whispers" have saved him from a life of sure boredom and self-destruction. "His well-timed words have redirected my path," Bill said, "rescued me from temptation and re-energized me during some of my deepest moments of despair."

On the grid that follows, note occasions in your own life when God's well-timed words have comforted you, rebuked you, provoked you to take action, invited you to experience greater freedom in some aspect of life and more. Record the whisper you received, the effect it had on you and what you did in response.

Whisper I Received	Effect It Had on Me	How I Responded
[example] "I still love you."	Comfort	Asked for forgiveness for my sin

Whisper I Received	Effect It Had on Me	How I Responded

RESPOND: *Thank God today for his whispering ways.*

If you have never stopped to thank God for communicating directly with his children — including you! — then do so now. In the space below, write a prayer of thanksgiving that you serve a God who craves frequent, consistent and *intimate* communication with you. Then, read it aloud to him as a way of closing your time together.

DIVINE INPUT
FOR THE DAY-TO-DAY

When Jesus is near, all is well and nothing seems difficult.
When he is absent, all is hard.
When Jesus does not speak within,
all other comfort is empty,
but if he says only a word, it brings great consolation.
Thomas à Kempis

What to Expect, Session 2

During session 2, you will meet Christ-followers from a variety of backgrounds and experiences who have discovered that God not only can intervene in major life decisions, but also in his followers' day-to-day routines. To prepare for session 2, skim the following two chapters from Bill Hybels's *The Power of a Whisper: Hearing God, Having the Guts to Respond*:

📖 Ch. 3, "Evidence from Everywhere"
📖 Ch. 6, "Light for Dark Nights of the Soul"

Opening Prayer

Focus your group on devoting this hour to God by praying the prayer below.

"God, here we are again, anticipating your presence, your power and your personal input into our lives. As we dive into this session's material, please help us corral our thoughts, channel our energies, still our bodies and focus only on you — who you are and what you want to say to each of us today. We love you, we live to serve you and we dedicate this time to you now. Amen."

Getting Going

As your group prepares to view this session's video content, briefly share your response to the following question:

What time of day are you at your best?

Video Notes

In the space below, record your observations regarding this session's video, as well as any personal promptings God lays on your mind and heart.

"As consequential as the big, life-altering whisper-led decisions can be, every bit as exciting is the day-to-day, ongoing conversation we're invited to have with a God who sees, who knows and who actually cares about the more routine aspects of our lives."

Bill Hybels

Group Discussion

After viewing the session 2 video, answer the questions that follow in full group.

1. As you watched the Christ-followers featured in this session's video explain the divine whispers they have received along the way, which stories resonated with you most on a personal level, and why? Share your insights with your group.

2. During the Individual Reflection portion of session 1, you were asked to note a few whispers you have received from God, along with the effect those whispers had on you. Review the grid you completed on pages 31–32; then, consider those whisper experiences through the lens of the three categories

that Bill Hybels addressed during this session's video: *whispers of assurance, whispers of admonition* and *whispers of action.*

Think about those times when God has provided *assurance* to you along the way. What was one difficult situation you remember walking through, and what divine assurance did you receive? Share your response with your group.

3. Regarding this idea of God providing assurance to his people, consider the myriad ways that he is described in the Old Testament. On the grid below, look up the following verses of Scripture and then fill in the role you find God playing there.

Scripture Reference	Role of God Described
Genesis 17:1–2	
Genesis 22:14	
Exodus 15:26	
Exodus 17:15	
Leviticus 20:7–8	
Judges 6:24	
Psalm 23:1	
Jeremiah 23:6	
Ezekiel 48:35	

Which of the roles of God has been most meaningful to you throughout your life? Explain why.

Which function noted on the grid on the previous page best reflects the role God is filling in your life today?

Why do you suppose God remains so committed to assuring his followers throughout the course of their lives by being their peace, their provision, their healing and so forth?

4. Next, think about the corrective or "admonishing" whispers you have received from God along the way. What words has God chosen to use as he has offered correction for your life? Select the words or phrases from the list below that apply to your experience, and then explain your response(s) to your group.

☐ "Stop!"   ☐ "Forgive."
☐ "Go!"   ☐ "Persevere."
☐ "Wait."   ☐ "Be patient."
☐ "Ask."   ☐ "Choose love anyway."
☐ "Keep asking."   ☐ "Trust me."
☐ "Enough!"   ☐ "Believe what you
                            know of me to be true."

Why do you suppose God often opts for issuing a corrective whisper rather than simply intervening in the course of his people's lives and thrusting his will upon them?

5. Moving on to the third category of whispers, when have you been prompted to *take action* by a divinely communicated prompting?

Whether the action seemed significant or trivial, how did it feel to be invited by God to participate in his plans for this world?

6. To bring these ideas down to the level of your daily routine, think about the twenty-four-hour period you just experienced. What did the day hold in store for you? Where did you go and who did you interact with? First, take a moment to jot down in the space below a few details about that day:

People I saw ...

Places I went ...

Tasks I accomplished ...

Decisions I made ...

Challenges I faced ...

Thoughts I entertained ...

Other notes about the day ...

Now, considering all that your day included, answer the following questions:

During that twenty-four-hour span of time, how frequently did you invite God to speak into your routine?

What distractions, assumptions or fears kept you from engaging God in your day with greater frequency, persistence and passion?

7. During this week's video segment, Bill Hybels said that while it was always easy for him to grasp the "transcendent" aspect of God's nature, it took him some time and effort to embrace God as immanent, as *near*. Which of the images below better reflects your current view of God? Place a check in the box that better fits.

☐ God as sovereign,
   lofty, "other than"

☐ God as intimate,
   accessible, near

How do the words of Psalm 139:7–10 (see shaded box) reinforce the idea that God is both sovereign over all and yet as knowable as your closest friend?

> "Where can I go from your Spirit? Where can I flee from your presence? If I go up to the heavens, you are there; if I make my bed in the depths, you are there. If I rise on the wings of the dawn, if I settle on the far side of the sea, even there your hand will guide me, your right hand will hold me fast."
>
> **Psalm 139:7–10**

8. Select the aspect of God's character you would like to focus on more intentionally between now and your group's next meeting. Then, in the space below, write out Psalm 139:7–10 in your words, as a prayer of commitment to God.

   ☐ His sovereignty over my life

   ☐ His proximity to me in my day-to-day routine

Giving the Whisper-Led Life a Try

Agree to engage in the following activity before your group meets for session 3 and to come to that meeting prepared to discuss your experience.

Ditch the Do-Not-Disturb lifestyle and put on a "spiritual Bluetooth" instead. As you plan your agenda for a particular day between now and your group's next meeting, ask, "God, what would *you* have me do today? Where would *you* have me go? Is there anyone whose path I need to cross? Anyone I should consider calling or visiting?"

If you are about to step into a meeting, say, "God, I know the people I'll be meeting with matter to you. Show me how I can serve them. Give me your words to say."

If you find yourself in a conversation with your spouse, your children or a close friend, ask, "Father, how can I love them well right now? Give me insight about how to show your compassion and care."

If you are driving from one place to another, turn off the radio, silence your phone and say, "God, this time is yours. Is there anything you'd like to speak to me about? I'm all ears."

Whatever endeavors you pursue these next few days, keep one ear attuned to heaven, asking God to whisper into your day-to-day life. Then record any divine input you receive on the grid below, as well as what you were doing when you heard God speak.

Whisper I Received	What I Was Doing When I Received It
[example] "Pray peace for your husband."	Commuting to work

Whisper I Received	What I Was Doing When I Received It

INDIVIDUAL REFLECTION
SESSION 2

Before you meet with your group for session 3, take some time on your own to review and pray through the big ideas from this session's content as well as the Sitting with the Subject Matter section that follows.

The Big Ideas

- God can intervene in life's major decisions, but also in our day-to-day routine.

- Throughout the course of our days, we can receive whispers of *assurance*, input that confirms God's promises of things such as his presence, his peace, his power, his provision and his protection in our lives.

- We can also hear whispers of *admonition*, corrective rebukes that encourage us to change courses or that save us from sure peril.

- God sometimes issues whispers of *action*, words that spur on his followers to meet a need or solve a problem in their corner of the world.

Sitting with the Subject Matter

READ: *Philippians 2:5–11*

Philippians 2:5–11 (see shaded box) details seven "voluntary demotions"[5] Jesus Christ took in order to manifest pure humility before his heavenly Father: he did not consider equality with God something to be grasped; he made himself nothing; he took on the form of a servant; he was made in human likeness; he humbled himself; he became obedient to death; and he endured the pain of the cross.

In large part, it was Christ's *humility* that opened his ears to the will of the Father. And it is that attitude we are told to reflect.

> "Your attitude should be the same as that of Christ Jesus: Who, being in very nature God, did not consider equality with God something to be grasped, but made himself nothing, taking the very nature of a servant, being made in human likeness. And being found in appearance as a man, he humbled himself and became obedient to death — even death on a cross!
>
> Therefore God exalted him to the highest place and gave him the name that is above every name, that at the name of Jesus every knee should bow, in heaven and on earth and under the earth, and every tongue confess that Jesus Christ is Lord, to the glory of God the Father."
>
> **Philippians 2:5–11**

REFLECT: *Are you humble enough to hear from God?*

Backing up a few verses, Philippians 2:1–4 describes real humility in a few simple phrases. *The Message* paraphrase says it this way: "If you've gotten anything at all out of following Christ, if his love has made any difference in your life, if being in a community of the Spirit means anything to you, if you have a heart, if you care — then do me a favor: Agree with each other, love each other, be deep-spirited friends. Don't push your way to the front; don't sweet-talk your way to the top. Put yourself aside, and help others get ahead. Don't be obsessed with getting your own advantage. Forget yourselves long enough to lend a helping hand."

On the grid below, note examples from your recent experience when you practiced five of the traits noted from this passage, like when you dropped your own preferences one night and invited your spouse to choose the restaurant instead; as well as times when you exhibited the exact *opposite* trait, such as when you disagreed with your friend over a trivial detail for a full five minutes, instead of just letting the conversation flow.

Aspect of Humility	Example of When I Practiced It	Example of When I Violated It
Being agreeable		
Being loving		
Being a "deep-spirited" friend		
Putting myself aside and helping others get ahead		
Lending a helping hand		

RESPOND: *Practice humility now.*

Review your entries from the "Example of When I Violated It" column on the previous page. In the space below, jot down names (or descriptions) of people who may have been harmed by your lack of humility during the experience you described. For instance, maybe you were abrupt with a server at a restaurant or selfish during a phone call with your mom.

Next, scan the list of people you noted above and consider who you can make amends with today. Ask God for direction here: Is there someone on that list who would be blessed by a sincere apology from you, a display of true humility on your part? Spend a few moments in prayer on this subject, and then write the person's name on the line below. Between now and your next group meeting, commit to manifesting a dose of humility with him or her by asking for forgiveness and seeking to rebuild the relational bridge.

_____

Learning to practice humility — a signature characteristic of the Christ-following life — will open you up to hearing from God with greater consistency and increased frequency, and it will position you to do exactly what your heavenly Father asks you to do.

PRACTICE, PRACTICE, PRACTICE

There is not in the world a kind of life
more sweet and delightful
than that of a continual conversation with God.
Brother Lawrence

What to Expect, Session 3

In this session, you will learn how to practice hearing from God as you would practice any new skill or discipline. To prepare for session 3, skim the following three chapters from Bill Hybels's *The Power of a Whisper: Hearing God, Having the Guts to Respond*:

- 📖 Ch. 2, "Our Communicating God"
- 📖 Ch. 5, "God's Written Whispers"
- 📖 Ch. 8, "When God Speaks through Others"

Opening Prayer

Focus your group on devoting this hour to God by praying the prayer below.

"Heavenly Father, if there is one thing we all want to get 'good at' in this life, it is hearing from you and following every syllable of instruction we receive. Thanks for being our omnipresent God, our faithful shepherd, our constant companion, our never-failing guide each day. We set aside every distraction and lean into you and each other for this hour. Show us what you'd have us learn about practicing your presence now. Amen."

Getting Going

As your group prepares to view this session's video content, briefly share your response to the following question:

What hobby, talent, ability or endeavor in life have you become good at because of your faithfulness to practicing it?

Video Notes

In the space below, record your observations regarding this session's video, as well as any personal promptings God lays on your mind and heart.

"You and I must commit ourselves to a few daily disciplines that help us get positioned to hear from God. Practice, practice, practice — that's what this is all about."

Bill Hybels

Group Discussion

After viewing the session 3 video, answer the questions that follow in full group.

1. What images come to mind when you hear the phrase "practicing the presence of God"?

2. Bill Hybels mentioned that the first way he tried to practice God's presence was by talking out loud to his heavenly Father in the car during his morning commute. What are a few of the ways that you have observed or heard about people practicing the presence of God?

3. Think about your own life experience. What types of things have you tried firsthand, in an effort to experience God's presence? Which of those attitudes or activities were most helpful to you and why?

"I know that for the right practice of it, the heart must be empty of all other things, because God will possess the heart alone; and as he cannot possess it alone without emptying it of all besides, so neither can he act there, and do in it what he pleases, unless it be left vacant to him.

"There is not in the world a kind of life more sweet and delightful than that of a continual conversation with God. Those only can comprehend it who practice and experience it; yet I do not advise you to do it from that motive. It is not pleasure which we ought to seek in this exercise; but let us do it from a principle of love, and because God would have us.

"Were I a preacher, I should, above all other things, preach the practice of the presence of God; and were I a director, I should advise all the world to do it, so necessary do I think it, and so easy, too."

Brother Lawrence

4. In this week's video segment, Bill Hybels talked about establishing a place where he could experience an enjoyable, repeatable meeting with God. In the same regard, where is *your* chair? Where do you regularly meet with God? Share your answer with others in your group.

5. Bill mentioned that each morning when he meets with God for twenty or thirty minutes, he follows the same set of practices:

- He settles on a passage of Scripture.
- He reads it and then reads it again, reflecting on those verses in a focused way.
- He jots down a few notes about what those verses mean to him.
- He asks God for additional insights from the text that are relevant to his life.
- He writes out a simple prayer of commitment to living based on the biblical concepts he has just read.
- He prays those words back to God, meaning them from the deepest part of who he is.

While it may vary from time to time, what does your "chair routine" typically include? Describe it to your group.

> "Married couples acquire an instinctive sensitivity to the quiet word or small gesture which others may never notice. Young lovers don't possess it. Beginners in prayer don't normally possess it about God either, but as the relationship with God develops, so does our instinctive judgment about what pleases him. There is no shortcut to the art."
>
> **David Pytches**

6. Spend a few minutes looking up and reading a few of the following verses. Based on the context you find there, what do you imagine was involved in Jesus' "chair routine" as he withdrew to spend time with his Father on a regular basis?

Matthew 14:23	Luke 4:42
Mark 6:31	Luke 5:16
Mark 6:45–46	Luke 6:12

7. How do you suppose a person can balance the routine or "task" aspect of meeting regularly with God with the goal of engaging in a *fluid and relational* way with him, as Christ did?

8. The practices we employ to order our fellowship with God are often referred to as "spiritual disciplines," and theologian Richard Foster is considered by many believers to be a leading thinker on this subject matter. His book *Celebration of Discipline* was named by *Christianity Today* magazine as one of the top ten books of the twentieth century and contains helpful distinctions regarding learning and implementing practices that promote intimacy with Christ.

   In that book, Foster includes twelve disciplines — four "inward" disciplines (Bill mentioned these when he talked about his morning routine), four "outward" disciplines and four that are "corporate" in nature. Take a look at the grid on the next page,[6] and then talk with your group about which disciplines you've tried to incorporate into your life along the way. What are some of the positive and negative experiences you have known as a result of your experimentation?

Common Spiritual Disciplines

Inward Disciplines	Outward Disciplines	Corporate Disciplines
Meditation: The ability to hear God's voice and obey his word	**Simplicity:** Recentering ourselves on the reality that all we have is from God and then making our resources available to those who need them	**Confession:** Claiming Christ's redemption by admitting to God and to others one's sin
Prayer: Communicating with God so that you can be aligned with his will	**Solitude:** The experience of inner fulfillment whether alone or in a crowd (as opposed to loneliness, which is inner emptiness)	**Worship:** To know, to feel and to experience the resurrected Christ in the midst of a gathered community
Fasting: Abstaining from food or other necessities for spiritual purposes	**Submission:** The ability to lay down the terrible burden of always needing to get one's own way	**Guidance:** The ability to receive knowledge of the direct, active and immediate leading of the Holy Spirit
Study: Renewing the mind so that old, destructive habits are replaced with new, life-giving ones	**Service:** The practice of radical self-denial in favor of meeting another's need	**Celebration:** Embodying a joyful spirit of festivity in daily life because of all that Jesus Christ has done for humankind

9. Which of the disciplines from the grid in question 8 appeals to you most during your present season of life? Explain why.

10. What types of distractions would you most likely face if you tried to incorporate that spiritual discipline into your daily life with greater intentionality?

11. As a commitment to God, write out Psalm 42:2 (see below) in your own words in the space that follows. Confess the things you have been "thirsting for" even more than God's presence, and invite him to be first on the list — perhaps for the first time in your life. Then, read your rewrite to your group, asking them to pray for you between now and your next meeting, as you seek to thirst first and foremost for God, by way of *practicing* his presence.

> *My soul thirsts for God, for the living God.*
> *When can I go and meet with God?*
> PSALM 42:2

"God intends the disciplines of the spiritual life to be for ordinary human beings: people who have jobs, who care for children, who wash dishes and mow lawns."
Richard Foster

Giving the Whisper-Led Life a Try

Agree to engage in the following activity before your group meets for session 4 and to come to that meeting prepared to discuss your experience.

Review your response to question 9 on page 58. On the grid below, circle the discipline you cited; then, on the righthand side, note one way that you can practice that discipline between now and when your group convenes again. Share your intentions with your group before you dismiss session 3.

Discipline I'd Like to Practice		How I'll Practice It This Week
[circle one]		
Meditation	Submission	
Prayer	Service	
Fasting	Confession	
Study	Worship	
Simplicity	Guidance	
Solitude	Celebration	

INDIVIDUAL REFLECTION
SESSION 3

Before you meet with your group for session 4, take some time on your own to review and pray through the big ideas from this session's content as well as the Sitting with the Subject Matter section that follows.

The Big Ideas

- We become what we practice; to become people who frequently hear from God, we must *practice* the presence of God.

- The first priority to practicing God's presence is to declare your "chair," the place where you enjoy a consistent meeting with him.

- There are many spiritual disciplines reflected in the life of Jesus Christ, such as meditation, prayer, service, worship and celebration. Practicing any of these disciplines, as Jesus did, will increase the likelihood that you will hear regularly from God.

Sitting with the Subject Matter

READ: *Mark 6:34–46*

Mark 6:34–46 (see shaded box) comprises the classic account of Jesus feeding a massive crowd with a meager five loaves of bread and two fishes. What is less well-known is that, according to verses 45 and 46, immediately after Jesus completed this grand act of service, he sent his disciples on their way, dismissed the crowd that had been gathered before him and "went up on a mountainside to pray."

> "When Jesus landed and saw a large crowd, he had compassion on them, because they were like sheep without a shepherd. So he began teaching them many things.
>
> "By this time it was late in the day, so his disciples came to him. 'This is a remote place,' they said, 'and it's already very late.'
>
> " 'Send the people away so they can go to the surrounding countryside and villages and buy themselves something to eat.'
>
> "But he answered, 'You give them something to eat.'
>
> "They said to him, 'That would take eight months of a man's wages! Are we to go and spend that much on bread and give it to them to eat?'
>
> " 'How many loaves do you have?' he asked. 'Go and see.'
>
> "When they found out, they said, 'Five — and two fish.'
>
> "Then Jesus directed them to have all the people sit down in groups on the green grass. So they sat down in groups of hundreds and fifties. Taking the five loaves and the two fish and looking up to heaven, he gave thanks and broke the

> loaves. Then he gave them to his disciples to set before the people. He also divided the two fish among them all. They all ate and were satisfied, and the disciples picked up twelve basketfuls of broken pieces of bread and fish. The number of the men who had eaten was five thousand.
>
> "Immediately Jesus made his disciples get into the boat and go on ahead of him to Bethsaida, while he dismissed the crowd. After leaving them, he went up on a mountainside to pray."
>
> **Mark 6:34–46**

REFLECT: *When do you regularly fellowship with God?*

The New Century Version translation of Mark 6:46 says of Jesus, "After sending them away, he went into the hills to pray."

Of all the people who have walked the planet, Jesus could have made the strongest case for being too busy to spend time in fellowship with his Father. He had miracles to perform, sick people to heal, lost people to find, wayward people to set straight, pious people to humble and humble people to embolden. He lived a *full* life. And yet even he prioritized a certain "pulling away."

Jesus' example invites everybody who loves him and is committed to following him to do the same. So, what's the truth about you? Do you regularly head for the hills, as Jesus did, even on the heels of your busiest days? Take a look at the "Respond" challenge on the next page, if you're ready to begin doing so today.

RESPOND: *Head for the hills, starting today.*

During the session 3 video segment, Bill Hybels said, "If you're an early-morning person, meet with God then. If you're a night owl, let that time be his. Whenever you're at your best, give that time to him."

If you're ready to prioritize meeting with God daily, first select a time of day from the images below that reflects when you are at your best.

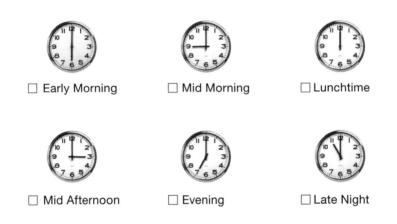

| ☐ Early Morning | ☐ Mid Morning | ☐ Lunchtime |

| ☐ Mid Afternoon | ☐ Evening | ☐ Late Night |

Next, commit that for one full week — every day for seven days straight — you will "head for the hills" and engage intentionally with your God. To help you seal your commitment, jot down answers to the questions that follow.

Where is "your chair"? Where will you meet with God?

How much time will you set aside for these meetings?

What will your "chair routine" look like for this week? What practices do you plan to employ?

How will you keep distractions at bay that threaten to trump your time with God?

What do you hope to gain as a result of devoting this time to God?

Consider setting an alarm on your PDA, your watch or your nightstand clock to remind you of this meeting each day. Whatever you need to do to keep your commitment, do it! Your faithfulness will prove fruitful as you increase your odds of hearing from God.

WIDE OPEN FOR GOOD

Hearing God — as a reliable, day-to-day reality for people with good sense — is for those who are devoted to the glory of God and the advancement of his kingdom. It is for the disciple of Jesus Christ who has no higher preference than to be like him.
Dallas Willard

What to Expect, Session 4

During session 4, you will be invited to become a more effective kingdom-builder by asking God to "rock your world" regarding the injustices that break his heart. To prepare for session 4, skim the following two chapters from Bill Hybels's *The Power of a Whisper: Hearing God, Having the Guts to Respond:*

📖 Ch. 7, "Promptings for Parenthood"
📖 Ch. 9, "Whispers that Change the World"

Opening Prayer

Focus your group on devoting this hour to God by praying the prayer below.

"God, we love your faithful leadership of our lives and value the input we've received from you during the past three sessions of this study. As we wrap things up today, we give you free rein to help us grasp the difference between craving your input regarding what matters to us and craving input on what matters to you. May what breaks your heart break our hearts too. And may great kingdom strides get made from this point forward because of our willingness to obey you."

Getting Going

As your group prepares to view this session's video content, briefly share your response to the following question:

What reality about our world at large troubles you most these days?

Video Notes

In the space below, record your observations regarding this session's video, as well as any personal promptings God lays on your mind and heart.

"Sometimes God wants to create a little discomfort for our comfortable lives."

Bill Hybels

Group Discussion

After viewing the session 4 video, answer the questions that follow in full group.

1. As you begin your group discussion, which aspect of this week's video segment was most impactful to you? Explain your response to the group.

2. During the video, Bill Hybels mentioned two levels of whispers that Christ-followers are likely to hear — whispers that offer comfort for the concerns of our own lives, and whispers that introduce *discomfort* into the equation, such as when God asked Bill to up the ante on his involvement in helping to bring about higher levels of racial reconciliation in his corner of the world.[7]

When have you been "discomforted" or disrupted in some significant way by a whisper or a prompting from God? Describe the experience to your group, including whether or not you chose to obey the whisper you received.

3. For many people, even the most disruptive whispers they have known from God began with a simple, straightforward task such as:

• "Ask the question …"
• "Watch the documentary film …"
• "Go to that learning group …"
• "Risk engaging in that relationship …"
• "Find the funding to take the trip …"
• "Read that book …"

Can you relate? When have you known a seemingly innocuous activity or baby step to catalyze a meaningful pursuit in your life?

4. At the beginning of this session, you were asked to name one reality about our world at large that troubles you more than any other these days. Note your response on the line below.

_____

Now, consider which "creature comforts" you most enjoy in life. Perhaps those include your morning Starbucks visit, the ability to dine at a favorite restaurant with your spouse every Friday night, a monthly golf outing or a house that is large enough to accommodate your entire family. On the grid below, note your top five; then share a few of your responses with your group.

My Favorite Creature Comforts
1.
2.
3.
4.
5.

As Bill Hybels mentioned during this week's video, although "world-rocking" promptings from God often start with small, innocent first steps, obeying them completely sometimes means sacrificing personal comfort at some point along the way. If obeying a whisper from God to help alleviate the societal ill you noted on the line in question 4 meant giving up your top five creature comforts, how would you respond to that whisper? Select the image below that might reflect your posture toward that divine input, and then explain your response to the group.

☐ **Open hands:** "Everything was yours to begin with, God. Whatever I need to let go of in order to obey your whispers, I release back to you now."

☐ **Closed hands:** "I worked hard for the comforts I enjoy, God. Isn't there someone else you can tap for this role?"

5. As you saw in this session's feature interview, one of the concerns Heather Larson felt as she sought to obey the whisper she received from God centered on how to juggle the demands of being a wife, a mom and an advocate for change within her local church. What practical concerns might make it difficult for you to keep an "open-hands" posture before God in receiving and then obeying challenging promptings from him?

To get you started, scan the list of categories below; then, share any thoughts that come to mind regarding these concerns (or others not noted) with your group.

Concerns about *family*	Concerns about *comfort*
Concerns about *career*	Concerns about *fulfillment*
Concerns about *money*	Concerns about *relationships*
Concerns about *time*	Concerns about *safety*
Concerns about *energy*	Concerns about *reputation*
Concerns about *health*	Other concerns ...

6. In response to Heather's practical concern regarding the well-being of her family, God whispered to her, "I love your family more than you do" and assured her that he would care for her family as she was faithful to walk in *his* will for her life.

To the one who worries about having enough energy to obey a world-rocking prompting from God, he says, "Come to me, all you who are weary and burdened, and I will give you rest" (Matthew 11:28). To those who worry about sacrificing personal comfort for the sake of following a whisper of God's, he says, "Do not worry about your life, what you will eat; or about your body, what you will wear. Life is more than food, and the body more than clothes" (Luke 12:22–23).

Throughout Scripture, we find God's promises of rest, of provision and more. What is one promise of God that could help *you* overcome a practical concern you might face as you seek to obey every whisper — even disruptive, world-rocking whispers — you receive? Offer your insights to your group.

7. Before moving on, spend a few minutes as a group intentionally and physically "unclenching your fists" before God. Place your books and pens down, open your palms toward heaven and offer a prayer to God, inviting him to break your heart regarding the issues that break his heart too. If you are ready for him to "rock your world" — if you're ready to be used in solving a societal ill — then tell him so and write out that commitment in the space below. Let the rest of your group hear you commit yourself to going God's way, not yours, with your life.

8. At the end of this session's teaching segment, Bill Hybels characterized his recent deep dive into the United States' need for immigration reform[8] as a "God-guided, whisper-led journey." What type of God-guided, whisper-led journey would you say you are on at the moment?

9. What do you imagine is true for Christ-followers who joyfully engage in a God-guided, whisper-led life?

"There comes a point in every serious-minded Christ-follower's life when the craving to know God's companion-ship trumps every other craving that can be known. There comes a point when nothing else will do."
Bill Hybels

Giving the Whisper-Led Life a Try

Before your group dismisses session 4, agree to engage in the following activity during the course of the next seven days.

In the book *The Power of Half: One Family's Decision to Stop Taking and Start Giving Back*, the story is told of the Salwens — Kevin, Joan, and their teenage kids Hannah and Joseph — a suburbanite family of four that posed a provocative question one day: "In a world where we often have excess, what would happen if we chose just one thing in our lives that we have enough of and gave away half?"[9]

The "one thing" they chose to split in half was their house. Feeling prompted to do some good in the world around them, they put their beautiful Atlanta home on the market, purchased a house exactly half the size, sold off all of the belongings that would not fit in their new living space and donated those dollars — plus the monies netted by the sale of the larger home — to a worthwhile charity that works to alleviate hunger in Africa.

The resulting dollar amount was significant, but that's not the point of the story. The point is that the Salwens intentionally carved out new capacities in their hearts, minds and lives for doing good in their world. They gave up something *meaningful* in pursuit of a higher collective goal.

And now, it's your turn.

Take another look at the creature comforts you noted on the grid on page 72. For the sake of freeing up space in your mind and heart that the voice and presence of God might fill, what is one "comfort" you are willing to cut in half this week? For instance, if you are accustomed to watching TV every night, decide that for one week's time, you'll cut that amount in half. And on the nights when you intentionally turn off the television set, devote that time to God. Ask him what is on his mind regarding the world around you, and how you might get involved. Pay attention to the baby steps he suggests in response — to place a call, to visit a learning group, to read a book. In the space below, note the "one thing" you'll cut in half this week, as well as the divine promptings you receive as a result.

What I'll cut in half…

Divine promptings I received …

INDIVIDUAL REFLECTION
SESSION 4

As you wrap up this "Power of a Whisper" experience, take some time on your own to review and pray through the big ideas from this session's content as well as the Sitting with the Subject Matter section that follows.

The Big Ideas

- Some divine whispers offer comfort for the concerns of our lives, while other, "world-rocking" whispers intentionally introduce a little *discomfort* into the equation.

- Obeying world-rocking whispers often involves personal sacrifice along the way.

- Despite the sacrifices involved, there is no greater satisfaction to be found on planet Earth than to joyfully engage in a God-guided, whisper-led journey.

Sitting with the Subject Matter

READ: *Isaiah 1:17*

In one succinct verse of Scripture, Isaiah 1:17 captures the priorities God intends for us to prize. "Learn to do right!" the prophet Isaiah exhorts. "Seek justice, encourage the oppressed. Defend the cause of the fatherless, plead the case of the widow."

Before moving on, jot down on the following grid a time when you have seen the priority that is noted get played out in everyday life. Maybe you observed a businessman stop on the street corner to offer lunch to someone who was evidently homeless and hungry. Perhaps you watched as friends of yours joyfully adopted a child who was growing up in foster homes. It could be you saw a group of loving Christ-followers rally around a woman who recently lost her husband to cancer. Whatever the circumstances, note a few of the ways you've seen God's priorities get brought to life.

God-Ordained Priority	What It Looks Like in Everyday Life
Learn to do what is right	
Seek justice	
Encourage the oppressed	
Defend the cause of the fatherless	
Plead the case of the widow	

REFLECT: *Do you practice God's priorities in a given day?*

You can't read of Jesus' ministry on planet Earth without gathering that he made a *practice* of living out his Father's prized priorities. At every turn, Jesus righted wrongs; infused the hopeless with hope; enfolded orphaned men, women and children in community; and saw to it that needy people in his midst had the resources they needed to thrive.

Can the same be said of you?

Would those who are closest to you — your family, your friends, the people you work with each day — testify to the fact that above all other priorities, your time, energy, money and creativity get spent on helping those who need a little help in this life?

Regardless of how you answer that question, *everyone* can stand to get better at prioritizing the things that matter most to God. If you're up for the challenge of living like Jesus lived, move on to the "Respond" section below.

RESPOND: *Prize God's priorities today.*

Choose a day this week to spend a few additional, uninterrupted moments with God. As you begin the day, complete the sentences that are started below as a way to invite God to speak to you regarding how your life might further his kingdom activity between now and when you rest your head on your pillow tonight.

- *God, as I think about the day that lies ahead, I anticipate ...*

- *My calendar says that today I am supposed to …*

- *As I think about how those tasks and plans square with the priorities you prize, I feel …*

Next, pose the following questions as a prayer to God, pausing for his input as you go.

- *I want to be open to your promptings today, God. Are there things you would change about the plans I've made for today? What tasks need to fall away? Which do I need to add to the list?*

- *In my heart of hearts, I want to "do what is right" today. What do I need to keep in mind as I pursue that priority of yours?*

- *Regarding "seeking justice," what will that look like for me today? Is there an injustice in my corner of the world that I'm not even aware of? Who do I need to talk to or where do I need to go, to uncover the need you'd have me meet?*

- *If I can be used today to encourage someone who is being oppressed—by another person, by systemic injustice, by their own bad choices—please show me exactly how. Who needs encouragement that I can bring, God? Will you open my eyes to their need?*

- *Are there people around me who feel orphaned, either by family, by friends, by you? Will you show me, God, who needs the protection and care only a loving Father can provide?*

- *And to the priority of pleading the case of the widow, would you please point me toward those who have lost loved ones and who are desperate for companionship and community?*

In chapter 10 of *The Power of a Whisper,* Bill Hybels writes, "If we were to boil down Christianity to its core, we'd be left with simply this: *relationship with God.* The living, loving God of the universe has spoken throughout history, and still speaks today — not just to pastors or priests, but to *anyone* who will listen. God will speak to *you.* No matter what spiritual condition you find yourself in, if you train your ear to be open to heaven, God will speak.

"A grand adventure with your name on it is on his lips. Tune your ear toward heaven, and he will direct your steps, accompany your path and celebrate your faithfulness one day."[10]

As you conclude your prayer time with God, tell him that the grand adventure he is willing to take you on is one you're excited to pursue. Nothing short of a God-directed, whisper-led life will satisfy the follower of Christ. Open your ears to hear from heaven, prize the priorities that God values most and just see what your heavenly Father will do in and through your life.

Oh! give me Samuel's ear,
An open ear, O Lord,
Alive and quick to hear
Each whisper of Thy Word;
Like him to answer to Thy call
And to obey Thee first of all.[11]

ENDNOTES

1. All Scripture references are taken from the NIV, unless otherwise noted.
2. For the full story, see 1 Samuel 3.
3. James Drummond Burns (1823–64), "Hushed Was the Evening Hymn," also called "Samuel" in some hymnals, from *Church Hymns with Tunes* (London: SPCK, 1874).
4. Bill Hybels, *The Power of a Whisper: Hearing God, Having the Guts to Respond.* (Grand Rapids: Zondervan, 2010), 50.
5. For more detail on these "demotions," see Bill Hybels' *The Power of a Whisper,* chapter 10, "Just Say the Word."
6. Adapted loosely from Richard Foster's *Celebration of Discipline: The Path to Spiritual Growth, 20th Anniversary Edition* (New York: HarperCollins, 1998).
7. The book Bill read during that "world-rocking" vacation is titled, *Divided by Faith: Evangelical Religion and the Problem of Race in America,* by Michael Emerson and Christian Smith (New York: Oxford University Press, 2000).
8. For more information on this subject matter, pick up Matthew Soerens and Jenny Hwang's book, *Welcoming the Stranger: Justice, Compassion and Truth in the Immigration Debate* (Downers Grove, Ill.: InterVarsity Press, 2009).
9. Kevin Salwen and Hannah Salwen, *The Power of Half: One Family's Decision to Stop Taking and Start Giving Back* (New York: Houghton Mifflin Harcourt, 2010), 226.
10. Hybels, 259.
11. Burns.

NAMES, NUMBERS, NOTES

Name	Contact Number

Email Address	Notes

Name	Contact Number

Email Address	Notes

_____

_____

_____

_____

_____

_____

_____

_____

_____

_____

_____

_____

_____

_____

_____

_____

_____

_____

_____

_____

_____

The Power of a Whisper

Hearing God.
Having the Guts to Respond.

Bill Hybels

"Without a hint of exaggeration," says pastor
and author Bill Hybels in his new book, *The
Power of a Whisper: Hearing God, Having
the Guts to Respond*, "the ability to discern
divine direction has saved me from a life of sure boredom and self-
destruction. God's well-timed words have redirected my path, rescued me from temptation and re-energized me during some of my
deepest moments of despair."

In *The Power of a Whisper*, vision is cast for what life can look
like when God's followers choose to hear from heaven as they navigate life on earth. Whispers that arbitrate key decisions, nudges
that rescue from dark nights of the soul, promptings that spur on
growth, urgings that come by way of another person, inspiration that
opens once-glazed-over eyes to the terrible plight people face in
this world — through firsthand accounts spanning fifty-seven years
of life, more than thirty of which have been spent in the trenches
of ministry, Hybels promotes passion in Christ-followers' hearts for
being wide open to hearing from God, and for getting gutsier about
doing exactly what he says to do.

Available in stores and online!

Share Your Thoughts

With the Author: Your comments will be forwarded to the author when you send them to *zauthor@zondervan.com*.

With Zondervan: Submit your review of this book by writing to *zreview@zondervan.com*.

Free Online Resources at

www.zondervan.com

Zondervan AuthorTracker: Be notified whenever your favorite authors publish new books, go on tour, or post an update about what's happening in their lives at www.zondervan.com/authortracker.

Daily Bible Verses and Devotions: Enrich your life with daily Bible verses or devotions that help you start every morning focused on God. Visit www.zondervan.com/newsletters.

Free Email Publications: Sign up for newsletters on Christian living, academic resources, church ministry, fiction, children's resources, and more. Visit www.zondervan.com/newsletters.

Zondervan Bible Search: Find and compare Bible passages in a variety of translations at www.zondervanbiblesearch.com.

Other Benefits: Register yourself to receive online benefits like coupons and special offers, or to participate in research.

ZONDERVAN.com/
AUTHORTRACKER
follow your favorite authors